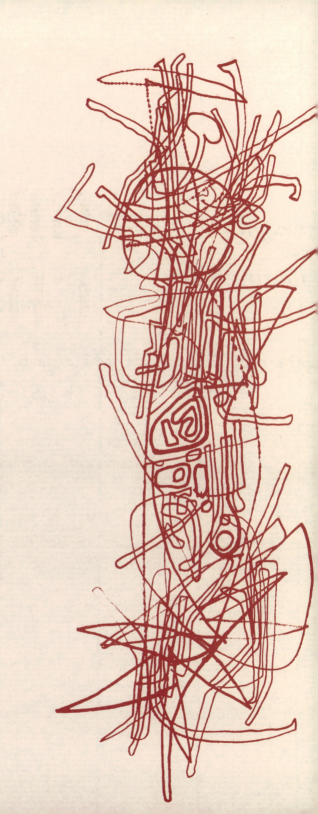

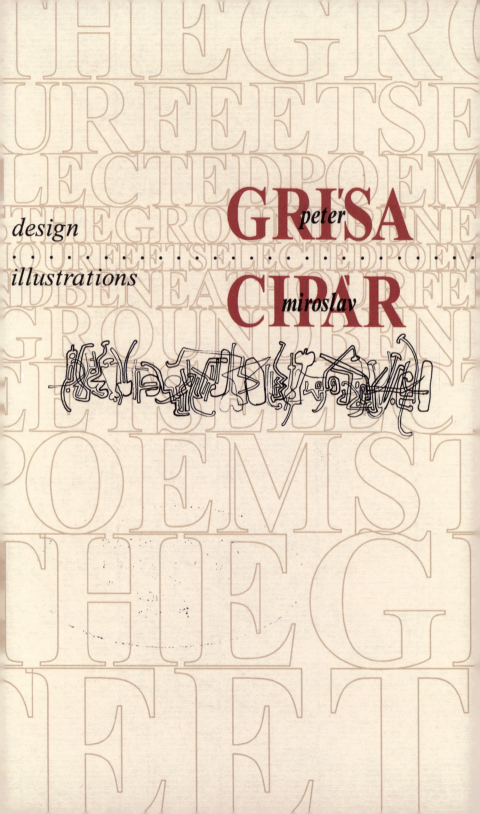

THE GROUR FEE TSE LECTED POEM THE GRO OUR FEE TSE LECTED POE NE DBENEA URFE GROUND EN POEMS T THE G EET

design

illustrations

GRISA *peter*

CIPÁR *miroslav*

translated by

foreword by

ewald **OSERS**

HOLUB miroslav

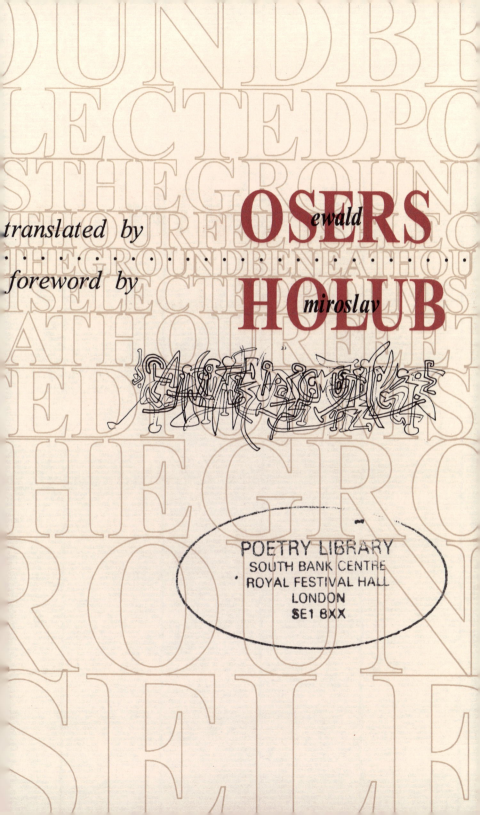

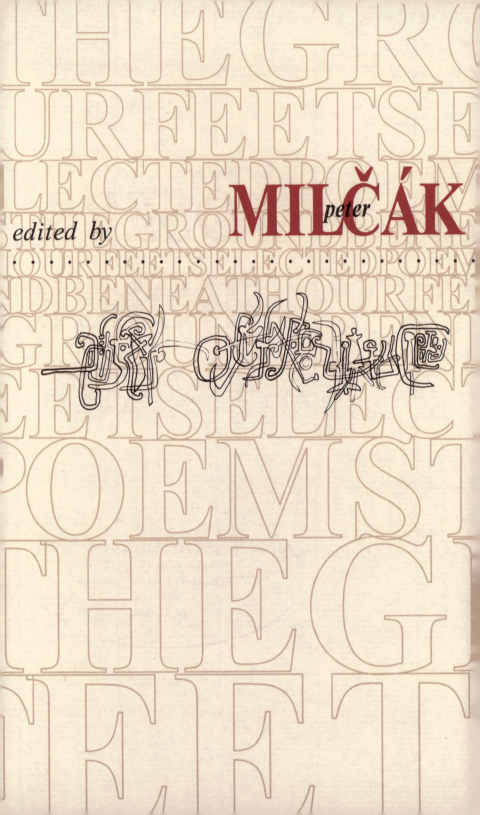

edited by

peter **MILČÁK**

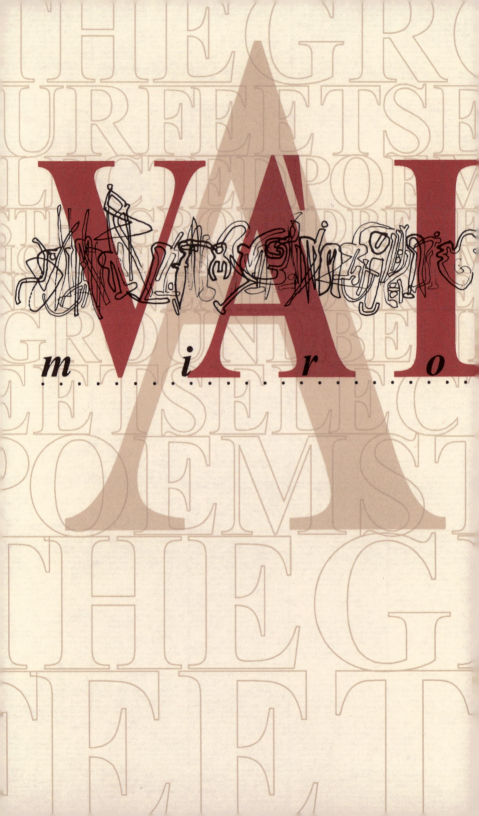

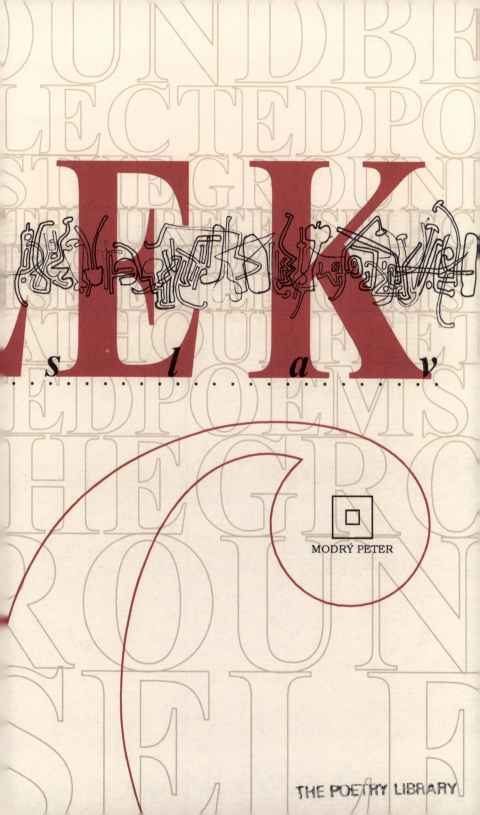

EK
s l a v

MODRÝ PETER

THE POETRY LIBRARY

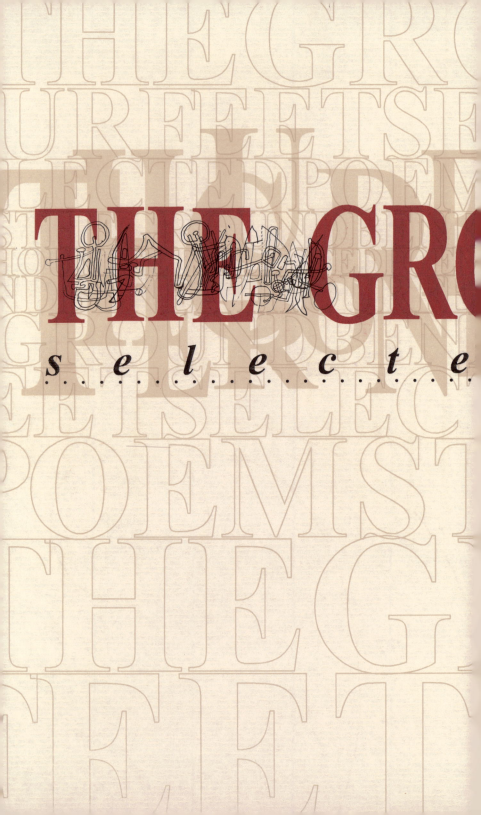

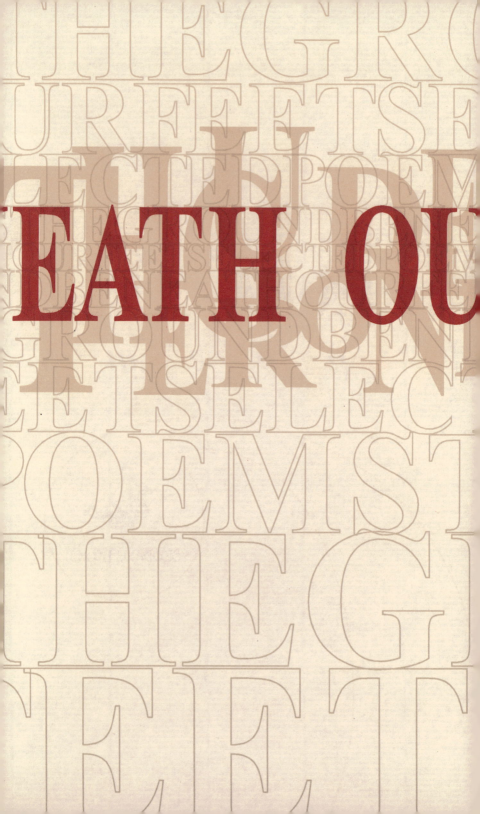

Selected by Ewald Osers and Peter Milčák

Edited by Peter Milčák

ISBN: 80-85515-37-7 Modrý Peter
        1 85224 377 5 Bloodaxe Books

First published 1996 in Slovakia by
Modrý Peter publishers
Ždiarska 6
054 01 Levoča.

First published 1996 by
Bloodaxe Books Ltd,
P.O. Box 1SN
Newcastle upon Tyne NE99 1SN.

Bloodaxe Books Ltd acknowledges
the financial assistance of Northern Arts.

Printed in Slovakia by Polypress, Levoča.

CONTENTS

FOREWORD
by Miroslav Holub

Miroslav Válek was born in 1927 and died, under tragic personal circumstances, in 1991. I saw him on several occasions from the 1960s onward and I always had the feeling that he was surrounded by tragic circumstances, even though he was one of the leading figures in the poetry of the sixties and even though from 1969 he was Slovak Minister of Culture. He invariably gave the impression of a man escaping rather than of one in a sunlit position.

He belonged to what the Slovak poet and critic Ján Štrasser has called the "first post-schematic generational wave", i. e. the generation which under the diluvial system of Stalinism either kept silent or, at the first signs of the Thaw, had enough sense to realize that one cannot at the same time be a poet and an obedient member of a Party in which the mastodons rule over the poets. That first post--schematic wave – in Slovakia mainly Milan Rúfus and Miroslav Válek, and in the Czech Lands the Květen (May) poets – rehabilitated poetry as a free art. This may not sound all that spectacular nowadays, but at the time it was like the invention of the wheel at the moment when the australopithecine hominids were beginning to climb down from their trees. In my opinion the invention of the wheel is still valid today when, in a framework of complete freedom

from Russians and Bolsheviks, but also from human solidari-
ty, the nth generation of post-schematic poets is busy
schematically inventing the square wheel.

Válek's poetry was and is clear and vivid, based on
images and events, often in an urban or otherwise
civilizational setting, it was and is a poetry, as far as
possible, of understanding the people, but at the same
time a poetry of a certain personal wistfulness, at times
of resignation, at others only of a sigh. His poetry was not,
even to the slightest degree, affected by his official post
in the 1960s, whereas his work as a minister certainly was
affected by his poetry – which is extraordinarily good
news for all questions about the sense of poetry. It was
very largely to Válek's personal credit that in the Czecho-
slovak culture of the eighties the mastodons began to die
out and those who "hear the distant galaxies and whose
hair is on fire" began to find not only a meaning but also
possibilities of publication.

Among his volumes of poetry the most memorable
were Dotyky (Contacts), Príťažlivosť (Attraction), Nepokoj
(Unrest), Milovanie v husej koži (Love with Goose-flesh).
The very titles are significant. In addition to writing his own
poetry he also translated some kindred Russians of his
own generation, such as Andrey Voznesensky.

A certain kind of unhappiness is the middle name of
poetry. Válek had to bear not only his own misfortune,
but also the collective misfortune of culture after the
Soviet occupation. He did what he could.

PARADE

It is eight in the morning,
the appletrees are in blossom, the dogs
                          are guarding the doors
and the winds are sleeping.
I didn't feel like thinking about rhymes,
I examine my conscience
like an old album with your photographs
which you no longer resemble
and which you have long forgotten.

Don't worry, I shan't trouble you for long.
All is correct,
order arms!

INCOMPREHENSIBLE THINGS

Incomprehensible things amidst us.
"What's this for and what is it like?"
A little wheel set turning between our fingers
                    performs its perfect motion.

But the watch isn't going.
An appletree in full bossom at the end of January.
But winter goes on.
A palpable feeling that someone's calling you.
But the street is empty.

And other things, too,
heard a hunderd times:
"... so he left her because he loved her ..."
"... they made life miserable for each other
because they couldn't bear being apart ..."

Where do these words come from, words
without logical justification,
without connection between one another,
incomprehensible
and odd?

Incomprehensible things,
let me be part of you,
pervade me with all senses,
let us touch each other
as a bow touches a violin.

Incomprehensible things,
you are within us.
Softly I utter words
and wait till you flare into life.

THE LYNCHED ONE

I dreamt that I was dangling on a rope,
without thoughts, without words, without strength.
A black face gazing at the stars.
A black face
                and all were scared of it.
But that face was looking at the stars.

Don't be afraid, the dead man won't move now.
It's only the wind,
it's only the wind that's rocking me.
Like the leaves on the trees,
the flowers,
the corn
and everything else.
Don't be afraid, the dead man won't move now.

Oh if only you walked past me
as though I had never been.
Oh if only you walked past me
holding hands,
looking at the starry sky ...
If only you were happy.

But everyone is afraid of me
because I am so alone
and so terribly lonely.
Why is everybody afraid of me
when I'm here so alone?

THE APPLE

The apple from the cupboard rolled to the floor.
Pack up your things and go.

She leaned back against the door
and with her eyes screamed:
For god's sake, please, no!
But I knew at once that I had had enough;
I got to my feet,
picked up the apple,
dusty and still green,
and put it on the table.
Incessantly she begged, she came to the table,
and cried.
She looked at me, wiped the apple,
and cried.
Until I said: Put the apple down and go!

The events unrolled as I had envisaged.
What does it matter if the sequence was different!
She opened the door,
I turned pale and said: Stay!
But she packed her things and went.

The apple from the cupboard rolled to the floor.

ONE MINUTE BEFORE GOING TO SLEEP

I saw a bird with gorgeous purple plumage.
My eyes are full of brilliant dissonances.
At night, when its wings have set the night aflame,
I am always alone,
torturing myself
with tears.
In my mind I invent
a moment with you among roses,
there I memorize the whole of you,
there I inhale you
till you say: Enough.

I know it's not permitted.

But wherever you touch my body
it becomes a clear vibrating note.
Stop it. Stop it now.
I am your music,
a tune you can't get out of your head.
You may whistle me
while thinking of others.

You're whistling me,
you're thinking of others.
I can't get it out of my head.
Let me go to sleep,
let me go to sleep,
fantasy purple bird.

BLINDING

How dark the night is!
By the river, in the park
the lilies are on fire,
silvery fishes flashing in the stream
and the ground shaking under stamping feet.

Let's go somewhere else!

Always the same –
the rolling of eyes,
wheels,
rising and falling,
concentrated and closed into themselves,
a slow movement to the peak and a fall.

How dark the night is!
To sleep with hands behind one's head
and think
of the splendid moment of leaving the earth
of the motionless body on the shutter!
Then even a casually heard word
                                    has a clear meaning,
then the sky is near,
the earth deep down,
the roots of trees largely improbable,
the face among the stars.

And everything only depends on the reflection!

In the cold rain
shortly before daybreak
they carried the cripple down the steps like a piano,
with wooden legs they crossed the treshold,

with their hands they groped in the freshly-dug
                              ground and found,
lowered it down,
foreheads facing each other, and bowed.

Now the moment
has come when you lie
where the diagonals of the room intersect,
you are that point,
that tremor above the cornfields,
you see everything while hiding
and rattle the posts of the horizontal world
                              in pointless anger.
The surface does not tilt, you won't see the sun in it,
nor the rain,
nor yourself.
Stagnant water, stagnant,
the fish on its bottom are burning.

But in that same direction, a glance further on,
women's feet walking behind the curtain
as if tapping on merry little drums,
men's feet
firmly, purposefully,
spin the World beneath them like a big bicycle,
on the town's pavement,
on the ocean's floor,
in the liquid metal of stars, in the glass of sand,
in ferns turned into anthracite,
everywhere, everywhere
the foofprints of man.

Two bare feet walking across my room.
Darkness hanging outside my window like a negative,
in vain do we look for ourselves in the picture,
night falls like a bird shot dead,
from left and right a wing of bombers,

water and air are rising to the sky,
the bell-tower sinks from the sky to earth.

To see Naples and then to die?
Why not visit Capri,
there's but one wedding night!
A naked man with a top hat is lying on the platform,
the bride is impatient, the train moves off,
ne pas se pencher en dehors,
nicht hinauslehnen,
è pericoloso sporgersi,
nenahýnajte sa z okien;
a dead man with a top hat is lying on the platform,
the bridesmaids are tittering stupidly.

Still the water rising to the mouth which speaks,
still the blurred, unsharpened
blade of the rain is submerged in the night,
beneath it a man with an apple jumps
                                        like a treefrog,
holding his big toe and shouting:
"And indeed we had occasion to convince
                                        ourselves of it –
the attraction of steel and of a child's face,
the attraction of bombs and the pavement!

But those faces fade in the albums
and vanish in the mind.

Until one day in the afternoon
full of humility
we sit down at the table,
open the album
from memory, reach into our memory –
nothing, nothing,
blank spaces,
as if you'd written on the window-pane: I love you

– and wiped it off with your sleeve,
as if they'd never existed
they're gone,
Tamara, Tatyana, Theodore, Theresa, Tibor, Tikhomir,
they're gone,
Magdalena, Malvina, Marcel, Mark, Monica,
they're gone,
Adam, Abel, Anna, Alena,
they're gone, but the steel remains.

Quiet and meek,
immaculate,
sovereign,
as the scythe before the rabbit
in the clover's green darkness
at daybreak,
when the white flag of cloud waves over the field,
blindingly bright,

like the body of a woman stepping out of the lake
in a nylon swimsuit.
The forest sounds off
with a thousand black clarinets,
but you wisely fall on your face.
Save yourself from contact,
save
the shape of a world long surmised.

Two bare feet walking across my room,
two bare feet which I don't see.
The sun is rising, a needle on the floor.
If I'd sound fingers I'd pick up the needle,
if I'd sound hands I'd lift up the world.
I turn my head,
always the same,
wheels
rising and falling,

concentrated and closed into themselves,
matter in motion.
I turn my head, but you're not here.

Tears and light,
emotion and dust.
The roar of the town enters into my pupils,
buildings and towers,
cranes and glass,
swimming pools and somersaults into the pool,
purple motorbikes with blondes in the sidecars,
but also forgotten things
and things only noticed by chance.
I myself am the town.

I have hands which polish crystals
and hands which bend sheet metal
I myself am the town,
a million runners
are running a marathon in me.

Through the walls of the aquarium
the world is dark green.
A motionless white fish hangs in the sky
                              like an airship.
But I stride through the water, through stones,
through the silent forest,
and an inch from the window,
from the spot where the clivias are just flowering
and a yellow bee flies out of the room,
there, closely following its flight with my eyes,
transparent and weightless I am reflected.

THE SENSITIVE ONES

The mirror should be behind one's back,
hands in gloves,
feet under the table.

Don't look now.
They are hunchbacks,
with one leg shorter than the other,
with one hand ending at the wrist.

They sit, they listen.
From the talk which doesn't concern them,
from the words which don't belong to them,
each selects his own:
... should have eyes at the back of one's head ...
... stepping out a bit lately ...
... work it out on the fingers of your hand ...

Oh why does the whole world touch on what
                                torments us?
Why do we have to carry with us our visible stigmata,

while a similar
and even worse deformity of the spirit
is hidden from everyone?

After death you will all have a beautiful hump.

STEEL–ROD BENDERS

On Vuk Karadžić Street
on the corner
two men are bending steel rods.
It is, in a way, poetic work.
The iron, like a verse, resists the human will.
But verse after verse,
verse after verse,
and you have a unique poem.
Above all those verses,
on the third floor
a blue-eyed punch-line settles in.
It will lovingly feel its four walls:
How firmly constructed it all is
and how much strength must go into such a wall.

If I'd had bigger muscles I'd have become
                              a steel-rod bender.

HEARING

Terrified
he jumps out of bed,
he hears the roar of distant galaxies,
the remarkably high-pitched whistle of falling stars,

he realizes
time and again
his abnormal sense of hearing.

Hands clapped to his ears he stands
                              in the middle of the room,
louder and clearer rings in them
the thunderous surf of darkness.
When at last he falls asleep
the birds awake in the lime-trees under his window.

I saw him again.
He was walking on the pavement
like a man entranced by something that's inside him,
he broke his step,
and at that moment suddenly
heard his feet rubbing against each other,
the crackle of sparks,
the confused trampling of urgent words.
He turned his head,
saw hair that was burning,
felt sweet burning vertigo
and nothing more.

Of course, that's all speculation, said the driver.
I honked like mad,
but he was looking at that redhead,
didn't move at all,
and now he's a goner.

Who'd have believed it,
such a fine-looking fellow
and deaf as a post.

WINGS

So this is summer. The blind people at Báhoň lift
their heads over the wall, over the barbed wire,
they observe the trains, long and sleek like their
                                                  whistle,
they pull up weeds and cough.
At Cífer a girl is sunbathing, her arms
above her head, the massive towers
                            of the petroleum industry
creep towards the railway line, they are all nodding
and thinking the same.

According to the calendar this is August 15,
                            St. Mary's, and 4 pm
the sun's in the beer, there's a storm in the air,
the park is full of lush greenery, and you're not here.
I've always said to you:
Come at the right time,
come at the roll of the drums,
exactly at noon,
when the swallows sign their autographs in the air
and things are silent,
come full of anger,
when you are sad, and when you feel like laughing.

Heads will again be at the windows,
                            things will be straight,
everything will again be in its place,
we'll spend the evening in your folks' garden,
we'll snap our fingers, the apricots will start glowing,
their yellow fires will again bend down to us:
Then, too, the grass was bluish and cool as a spring,
a polka-dot rain like a tie hung down
                            obliquely from the clouds,

a flash of lightning began in the sky
                        and reached down to our kiss.
When that storm had been going on for some time,
knocking too loudly at the tin-sheet of thunder,
you said they would be looking for you ...

In the darkness I saw you streak across the yard.

That night the earth moved in its bearings,
all the stars were born,
the universe shook like a young lamb
and sought its centre.

The day after the creation of the world
                        the radio was playing,
people walked about rooms,
they walked, they talked,
they crumbled bread,
they made their spoons ring,
ring loudly,
but no one took any notice of your wings,
transparent feather-light wings.

We caught you, blindness of mature age,
it made us feel good,
and what happened happened.
That same Saturday, after fifteen years
a chap called Abel,
with whom I used to buy tickets for football matches,
told me that we'd lost out long ago,
that we've no wings whatever,
and that's a sad thing.

So I'm at home, holding on to the earth,
the earth that goes with me everywhere,
my earth, the plain of insignificant people,

of workers from the Kovosmalt factory
                    and the atomic power plant,
who six days of the week deputize for god
in the building of the world that's so shamefully
                    behind schedule
because all the saints
responsible for good order had taken bribes
and the mills of god had ground for the bosses only.

I'm at home. Eyes full of earth and hands full of
                    hands I'm growing
inward into myself.
Summer into air. Summer at every step.
Summer yellow as a wasp forever behind us.

Behind the bloody line of the horizon,
in God's gardens,
where according to the theologians Paradise lies,
where the devil's anger simmers
                    and pomegranates explode
and angels with gas masks
with flaming swords in their hands close
                    their blind circle,
man's fate is written.
But we, now that we know
that mass is only a particular form of energy,
have more easily spread our wings,
we move with equal ease in space and time
and we know that this place is here with us,
                    on earth.

Our bequest to you,
delightful ones, dreamed-of ones,
                    springing from our blood:
Think of us,
we were your destiny

just as you are the destiny of those
who after you will cross
the border line of life.

THE GROUND BENEATH OUR FEET

Knee-deep mud, and rain enough to drown.
Grey and leaden skies are falling down.
Lonely raven, flying round and round:
where is dry land still, where solid ground?
Ground to you is that to which you're clinging.
In the taverns silent men are drinking.
Drinking for Dutch courage, for their fears to drown.
Like a goose the tavern's rocking up and down.
Heads like chunks of bread lolling on the tables.
Solemn yellow candles flickering in chapels.
Numb and heavy water falling from the sky.
Yet the ground keeps silent, ploughed for those who die.
Faces turned away, tears wiped away, but
the ceaseless lament.
As it was in the beginning so it shall be time without
end.

*   *   *

One moment before falling asleep,
                         in time's total immobility,
facing you I am retreating backwards.
There the green sun of my childish drawings sleeps,
a three-legged dog talks there
                         with a clear human voice,
an inky thrush flutes softly on my blotting paper.
The true appearance and meaning of things emerge.
Far away, but everything's as it used to be,
untouched and pure, for everyone has his childhood
locked away with a key that is lost forever.
At difficult moments we come here,
knock at the door and command: Open up!
But the house on its magpie's legs does not stop.

Only a mute thrush, startled, flies straight into the sun.
Locked. Locked for a million years, maybe forever.

That is why, when we reminisce aloud,
our children cry and say to us: Stop it!
Stop your terrible story in which everything is sad.
Sad dreams, sad dawns, sad sinking stars,
torn from the night sky.
Thus death would stalk about, setting light to the blue
                    fires of alcohol in the heads of the fathers.
The round black loaf of bread, hanging above
                        the mouths like some fantastic moon
but waning a hundred times faster,
and the desparate orbits of the children's eyes
            following it to its complete disappearance.

Oh sweet mother tongue and the bitterness of two
                words essentially innocent; Mummy, give.

What kind of sound is produced by a tear that falls
                in absolute silence, clear, transparent?

Head in our hands we reflect if it was true.
Where are you now, vast plain with the landowner's
                                        traps
marking your face like measles?
Where are you now, vast plain of farm-hands,
                            muddy and weary,
plain of vagabonds and village idiots,
humiliated and stripped naked,
shaking under the head-scarf of poverty,
before the eyes of a just god
bought for three bags full of authentic indulgences?
We have forgotten you,
we have forgotten you all,
hands buried alive,
hands without work, without real meaning, useless.

In the miraculous darkness of a July evening,
in the tense silence before the ripening of the fruit,
at the laying of the last slate on the roof
                                    of your house,
at the moment when you close your eyes before
                                    going to sleep,
all of you who praise your day,
call on the waters.
Call on the waters that have flowed away,
say to the waters in whatever form:
Return, ancient rivers, and flow back through your
                                    old courses.
Ripples on the surface, contract all the way
                to the fatal fall of the suicide's body.
Turn green, blind eyes of wells,
wipe clean your mirrors upon which is written:
                        disease, poverty and hunger.
Blood-sweat, spring up from the depths
                                    of the ground,
do homage to the hands which sowed you into it.
Take pity, oceans,
return your salt to the tears of women and mothers
                who broke down beneath life's burden.

Unite, waters past and waters primordial,
bear witness to the living
who, when they touch the sun,
need the certainty of knowledge,
a solid point,
the ground beneath their feet.

THE KILLING OF RABBITS

On Sunday after breakfast,
when the air is about halfway to ice,
the thin flutes of the mice are whistling
                                    in the chimney,
on Sunday after breakfast
to walk over fresh snow
to the cages.

Pull off the gloves for the rose feast.
Impale them on the fence
like freshly severed palms
and smoke through the door.
And then insert the hungry hand
and with smoke in your teeth utter sweet words,
caressing and gentle,
a touch of pity,
then a firm grab of the skin,
lifting it from the warm straw.

On Sunday after breakfast
sniff the ammonia.

For a while hold it head downwards,
watch the ears turning dark red,
gently stroke its back,
exhale, carry it off
and abruptly strike the back of its neck
                                    with the right hand.

Once more in your palm feel the effort
of a now useless leap,
feel a weight in your hand,
sweet taste on your palate,

hear the rabbits' heaven open
and fistfuls of fur falling from it.

Vinnese blue,
Flemish giant,
French lop-eared,
Czech piebald,
and even the bastards of no matter what blood,
they all die equally swiftly
and soundlessly.

On Monday with blue under your eyes keep silent,
on Tuesday reflect on the fate of the world,
on Wednesday and Thursday
bring out the steam engine
and discover the stars,
on Friday think of others,
and especially of blue eyes,
all week long feel sorry for orphans
and admire flowers,
on Saturday step pink from your bath
and fall asleep on her lips.

On Sunday after breakfast
kill a rabbit.

SENTIMENTAL CHRISTMAS

This is our happy Christmastide.
Hundreds of orphans freezing like black crows
while white-spumed oceans rush up to enclose
us and its thirsting roots torment the sun.
Grey, heavy stars of melted lead we cast
together into clear transparent water
while round the house a pack of wolves moves past.
And you're my silver-paper love,
let's eat some dark-gold mountain honey.

I walk around you in a circle.
I scrutinize you hard in yellow wonder.
Mad violins and howl of wolves,
the house resists, it won't go under.

For you, my love, mimosa blooms and thunder!

Love me!
Be moist as the night,
be like a bottomless well!
I'm burning like the sun
and thirsting
for you.

The waters have risen, the stream cracks its whip,
the drowned laugh loud beneath the ice.
My head is all but dropping on the table,
I'm cut by a sickle-moon above the gable,
a flash of blood,
a sabre,
the garden's a pyre.
And in the stove I hear a merry devil
fanning the fire.

This is our happy Christmastide,
the music of the bells,
the quiet night,
our home.

Reddish-brown fleas jump from the fire,
my hand is itching for that delicate neck.
The room turns blue like metal being welded.
And bracelets
strangle her white wrists.

But no,
not really.
Her slender hands with hesitant tinkle,
two meek little lambs,
retreat now from my body.
The firmament's extinguished.
The earth has flown away.

Allelujah,
allelujah,
I'm saved already.

Ding! Dong!
The whole town's brass like a bell.

Ah, that youth with its pains,
the crimson world!
She wept and cried.

Ding, dong, dong!

It was an unbelievable run.
She was still on my tongue as sweet as gingerbread.
It was a white Christmas,
with black snow
falling.

CONTACTS

From early morning telegrams have been arriving
                              at your address,
a flood of letters is swamping the house,
all the telephones in the district are ringing at once.

It's nothing, really it's nothing,
it's just me calling you all the time,
I'm re-establishing a cut-off connection.
What a good thing they believed me
at the post office and the telephone exchange,
that I'm sending a million greetings to you
that I'm begging you a million times:
Forgive me, but this is terribly important,
I don't know if I am coming or going,
I am most frightfully in love with you,
leave everything just as it is,
leave the water burning in the bathroom,
leave the gas running in the kitchen,
leave the frantic mirrors revolving in the living room,
and take the next train,
join me out here on the vast plain!
You shall be met off the train by seven black horses,
each with a star on its forehead,
the jasmine shall bloom,
the pollen fall from peach-trees
more delicate than your Soirée de Paris powder.

Hurry – at the corner
the evening's already blowing its horn,
                              painted blue like an ancient motorcar,
the urban sun, a scratchy played-out record,
                              is slipping below the horizon,
but our burnished copper casserole is setting
                              brilliantly:

as it touches the Earth you can hear it all.
The black bull at the co-operative breeding station
has finished his lyrical intermezzo in a velvety bass,
the plain is dropping on its knees and settling down
                                                    for the night.
The time has come to take off one's boots,
a stamping as at a ceremonial march-past,
for in every house here are lads tough as steel
and the sound has plenty of room here
                                        to gather speed,
so you need only switch off the radio
and you'll hear what everyone's dreaming ...

Dreaming of
glass,
stone,
metal,
the caress of a hand,
a bent forefinger tapping on the window,
a quick smile that you were waiting for,
ineffable things are seen in dreams,
miraculous things are seen in dreams,
miraculous things, things as plain as a snowdrop,
I dream of your head on my shoulder
and my eyes deep in your eyes,
we both dream,
dream,
and everything is just as in a magician's hat.

Night, a black hat with a broad rim, is turning upside
                                        down at dawn.
And now you see how corporeal some dreams are.
Nervously the fingers of TV aerials puncture the night,
new houses in columns of two are quick-marching
                                        into the villages,
the morning is stuffy like a dance-hall after a ball,
a solitary sad crow in the sky is circling like a fan,

fat ears of corn are swooning in amazement
as the local herald rooster hoarsely calls:
                                    Reaping time!
                                    Reaping time!

Momentarily the village is empty like a blown-out egg.
Only an old mother is sitting at her door, singing softly:
            "Went out to sow oats
            in their tattered coats ..."

The poor old mother, old and blind!
She used to milk the cows at Herz's dairy farm.
She used to pray for a long life and a happy death.
Her life went by like the crack of a whip
                                    – and hurt as much.
And now she no longer knows what kind of world
                                            this is.
She doesn't remember the names of her
                                    grandchildren,
she starts in panic when there's laughter in the house,
the evening wafts to her the strange foreign smell
                                    of diesel fumes,
but the earth she takes between her fingers
                                    is still good.
It's the same earth as long ago ...
The crêpe-de-Chine dress, the sixteen-yeard-old,
                    and the long braids have gone
but the plain has remained, the plain is eternal,
even though it now breathes more quickly
                                    and audibly.
Roast geese still fly, as in the fairy-tale,
                                    to feasting tables,
the vulture takes off vertically, like a rocket,
in autumn lilac-coloured rain falls on the gardens,
the heavy drops of plums drum on the weary ground.

The plain yields its fruits, it has no more to say,
                                                it is silent.
Sleepy,
blinded with molasses and sugar, it puts on its
                                        padded coat.

The first snow falls on St. Martin's Day.

ODE TO LOVE

At just that moment between night and day,
when the Earth spins on a beer-bottle,
when even hell at last reposes,
the devils' flea is already drunk
and the devil of fleas sleeps in the feathers
                                        of black hens,
when the dust flies
from the ears of grain,
when poppy-seed is ground behind dull eyes,
when the darkness is blackest in the crotch,
at just that moment lying on her back
the woman sorrowfully whispers water,
spells smoke:
What, when, how often and with whom ...

Something's knocking in the egg.
Someone's voice is begging "Come in!"

In some head a head is rolling,
                            some man is hanging there
in the noose of a little word.

A rat's tooth is gnawing away at the sky.

Multiplication of things.
Crashing of ice-floes.
Caresses setting the world ablaze.
Love-making with the goose-flesh
of amazement.

Night, damp as after the copulation
of stars.
Love like the sky.
And a moon like a fist.

An air that grinds the coarse potato chips.

The angry music of glass.

And dark and dark, right to the naked bone,
almost a white glare ...

... God constructing a new machine
from a body's spares.

ODE ON ETERNITY

Some day of some summer, when the bees
tune the piano in their hives,
when water isn't at home to anybody,
when rain
longs to become nothing
again.

There's something more in things than only music,
when winged men
fly out from the workshop.
Enter it and
you'll become immortal!

Of course: the worms
– they spoilt it all!
They wallow in the clay
and wind the clocks in the trees.

And a tree leans over
and retreats into autumn.
Abandoned. Alone.

And it would trade eternity for sympathy,
for a kind word,
for anybody's face
to gaze on.

A thunderclap. Applause
of pigeon's wings.
The fall of a downed star.
Fall of a star.
Fall
without beginning and without end.

To hear the lead shot flying round God's head
and the snow falling on the soul of the elder-tree
as on a miser's soul.

CALENDAR

January, February, March, April, May
and other moons.
Come, love me for a while as if you meant it!
Listen as from the gullet of the night
blood squirts and drains.
Let time pass imperceptibly
and let the seasons change
in the duration of a single kiss,
let the bright fire in the stove rejoice.
Detach me from your lips
and blood-red like a cherry pip
plant me beside you.

If only grass and soil could give me root.
I am the boy who collided with a star,
I'm bringing you the blue of the sky,
the blue bruise under your eye.
You're good for me. You make me feel my depth.
Oh yes, I was in heaven.
                    I drank the rainbow's colours!
And now to rest, like clay under the waters!
They've turned the lights off.
                    They've unleashed the dogs.

Before you fall asleep put me under your pillow,
I'll gently grow into your hair.

The night is hanging like a bat head-down.

Put me in store as if I were a pear.
And keep me until Christmas, at the least!

AUTUMN

Go mad
or drink yourself to death.
Autumn is placing its damp hands on your shoulders,
asking for a light,
on autumn's sleeve a mouse is sitting
and autumn begs:
"Don't go away, but buy it rubies."
You refuse, so it buys you instead.
And now you can't get rid
of those furtive steps behind you
and within you that departure without reason
– and, in effect, where to?
Even while you're asleep
you can hear autumn winding up its clock,
angrily smoothing out its velvet,
afraid it might be late.

The train whistles,
over the yards now flies
the last square root of a bird.
Write it all down, you foolish accountant –
that you had lots of luck,
great fear
– and all that gold
in your pockets!

Write it all down,
the autumn's losing it for you.
The lights have gone out in the wine-cellars.
Now darkness for six months.
Prodigals
returning home with rubies.
Everything's clear:
The trees have cast anchor,

deep in the clay the clanging of the chains,
under the bridge the water's lapping.
So heavy is the word we cannot understand
that you begin to be afraid.

Now someone here is clapping.
And from hand to hand
autumn is pouring its coins.
And the sold children go to bed.

WINTER

In winter everything's cleaner and whiter. There's snow
and whiteness everywhere, till it hurts.
Winter alone combs the streams of its pitch.
Storm flays the trees like a razor-blade,
somewhere in me a wild beast howls.
Then comes the night,
turning and wiping the moon's lens,
and by the morning it has snapped it from all sides.
But this is now a dark-blue winter.

My winter is white. Occasional winds
hardly bark from under the doors.
My winter is good.
Let's throw away
the old hat of melancholy
and run bareheaded down to the steep bank.
My winter is tenderness,
the winking of stars
and the sheer sparkle of snow.

There are still other winters. One that I remember:
the rosy winter of your body.
And as I filled my lungs with that rosy winter
the old white winter began to bore me.
I travelled through my winters like a submarine.
A gasp of air into my lungs, sharp as a knife!
I want to hear the crack of quartzite joints,
I want the coarse hair of a black winter
winding around my finger.
Let ordinary, human blood,
red blood,
drip on the snow.

THE HISTORY OF THE GRASS
For Oldřich Mikulášek

You should have seen it –
that phosphorescence!
That meadow, glowing like a wristwatch
showing springtime!
Its legs are feeble still,
its muscles will ache
but already on the hillside flashes its green cabriolet,
O, acceleration of grasses!

And chlorophyll!
And vernal sprouting!
And two hundred thousand other kinds of nonsense!
Your head's not spinning yet
but the grass is already starting the next lap.
Sing something gay,
sing something, quickly!

Frightened like deer
we're ageing before the grass's eyes.

And now it is no longer the racing car,
the thunder of vernal motors,
the frenzy of the grandstands!
It's just a sad vehicle with beer
from which they've flung
a green bottle with froth in its throat,
young foals,
grasshoppers
imitating a gallop.

One – two
pick up those legs
squad: sing!

And thus man lived to reach a thousand years.
He just had to run,
overtake with froth in his throat,
nobody asked him:
"Why" or "Where to?"

And who asked the grass which way it was growing
                                            and why?
Who asked about its inner life?
Who translated as much as a blade of grass
into human speech?
Nothing, except fire and rain.

And the grass works:
above the moles' passages,
above the grave,
above the grave,
it hears the lament of the sea,
the murmur above the aorta,
it transforms
the sun's conflagration,
the water's madness,
it transforms
dead things into living things,
it torments itself with itself,
it seeks their proper forms.

These have been written:
the history of wars,
the history of stamp-collecting and football.
The history of grass has not been written by anyone.
From grass's point of view this is irrelevant.
Its history is long and continuos.
Express trains ply in it
and horsemen bite their horses' manes.
A head with golden hair sinks into it
and many a cock has lost its comb in it.

Oh yes, it knows the errant stars!
Grass knows what leads to blood.
Its memory holds all those summertime loves,
adulteries
and brutal murders.
But grass is patient
and sensitive.
Grass covers everything.
It keeps its silence.

Do not look down on it condescendingly.
Grass knows what gives a toothache to the dead,
it knows all about life and death.
It has an accurate record of hopes and tears.
It has worked out your definitive form,
it has underlined you in green
and now waits.

One day I shall understand everything
and will reveal to you the secret connections
                                        of things.
Come,
let's go out into the darkness
to hear the birthpangs of the grass,
the fierce spasm of the roots,
the bursting of the cells,
the bubbling of the sap.
Now I undestand everything
as though I were a blade of grass myself.
Place your hand on the back of night,
and listen carefully to what I say to you:

Nothing, except fire and rain!

This book was given a subsidy by the National Centre
for Slovak Literature in Bratislava, Slovakia.

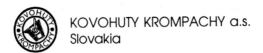 KOVOHUTY KROMPACHY a.s.
Slovakia

The book was published with the support of Open
Society Fund in Bratislava.